This Health Journal Belongs To:

Name:	E-Mail:
Address:	Phone:
City/State/ZIP:	

My Dog:

Name:	Gender: M / F
Breed:	Coat Color:
Birth Date:	Eye Color:
Spayed/Neutered: Y / N	Chip ID:
Favorite Game:	Favorite Toy:

Dog Photos

Emergency Clinic:

Name:

Phone:

E-Mail:

Address:

Veterinarian:

Name:

Phone:

E-Mail:

Address:

Groomer:

Name:

Phone:

E-Mail:

Address:

Dog Sitter:

Name:

Phone:

E-Mail:

Address:

Dog Medical Information:

Allergies:

Illnesses:

Injuries:

Blood Type:

Identifying Marks:

Attack Triggers:

Anxiety Triggers:

Behaviour Issues:

Feeding Info:

Notes:

Vaccination History

Date:	Vaccination:	Age:	Veterinarian:	Next Due:

Vet Visit History

Date:	Reason for visit:	Veterinarian:	Notes:

Vet Visit History

Date:	Reason for visit:	Veterinarian:	Notes:

Vet Visit History

Date:	Reason for visit:	Veterinarian:	Notes:

Vet Visit History

Date:	Reason for visit:	Veterinarian:	Notes:

Made in the USA
Middletown, DE
08 November 2022

14414941R00064